For my father, whose picture-making first
inspired my own

First U.S. edition 2019

Library of Congress Catalog Card Number pending
ISBN 978-1-5362-0853-5

19 20 21 22 23 24 TLF 10 9 8 7 6 5 4 3 2 1

Printed in Dongguan, Guangdong, China

This book was typeset in IM FELL Double Pica
and QumpellkaNo12.
The illustrations were done in
ink and colored digitally.

BIG PICTURE PRESS
an imprint of
Candlewick Press
99 Dover Street
Somerville, Massachusetts 02144

www.candlewick.com

# Animal Journeys

**Many animals, both great and small,
make incredible journeys.**

Some, like reindeer, migrate to find food. Others, like Christmas
Island red crabs, travel to find the right environment
for the next generation to survive in.

Animals make journeys in water, by air, across arid deserts, and over
freezing pack ice. In *Animazes*, you can follow the migrations
of fourteen very different creatures.

Can you find safe paths for them all?

# How to use this book

Each maze in *Animazes* has at least one safe path to follow. But there
are also a few perilous dead ends, so be careful! Trace each animal's
journey with your finger and learn all sorts of fascinating
facts along the way.

The beginning of
each maze is marked
with a red flag.

The end of each
maze is marked with
a checkered flag.

# In Animazes you will meet:

**Christmas Island Red Crabs**
These bright-red crustaceans scuttle to the sea to lay their eggs.

**Wildebeest**
Huge herds kick up the dust as they gallop across East Africa.

**Humpback Whales**
These mammals swim thousands of miles to give birth to their calves in the warm seas near the equator.

**Reindeer**
Vast herds of reindeer migrate to the Arctic tundra in summer.

**Monarch Butterflies**
One hundred million monarch butterflies fly south to California and Mexico every winter.

**Mali Elephants**
These elephants travel to find water in the Sahara Desert.

**Ruby-throated Hummingbirds**
These teacup-size birds make a dangerous journey over the Gulf of Mexico.

**Alpine Ibexes**
Acrobatic ibexes are cliff-hopping goats that migrate up mountains in summer.

**Antarctic Krill**
These shrimplike creatures rise and sink daily to avoid predators.

**Straw-colored Fruit Bats**
These bats swoop through Africa's night skies to find their favorite food.

**Polar Bears**
Polar bears migrate to follow seals, their main food source, which swim among moving pack ice.

**Rockhopper Penguins**
These nimble penguins scale sheer cliffs to find a safe place for their eggs.

**Sockeye Salmon**
These champion swimmers swarm in rivers and can even jump up waterfalls!

**Arctic Terns**
These intrepid birds fly from the Arctic to Antarctica and back again every year.

# Christmas Island Red Crabs

Christmas Island, in the Indian Ocean, is home to one of the most colorful migrations in the world. Every rainy season, the island's 40–50 million red crabs journey from the central rain forests to the coast, where they mate and lay their eggs.

Migration begins around November, when the monsoon rains arrive.

**Can you find the red crabs' path to the sea?**

Crabs require moisture to survive. They stop migrating if the rains stop.

Cars are a major hazard to red crabs. Some roads on the island even have crab tunnels running underneath them.

It takes adult crabs around a week to get to the coast.

As soon at the crabs get to the sea they dip into the water to replenish fluids and salts.

The crabs mate in burrows near the coast. Males then return to the rain forests. Females wait twelve to fourteen days until their eggs are ready.

The crabs are able to climb the tall, steep cliffs that surround Christmas Island.

The phase of the moon is important for red crab migration. Female crabs release eggs during the last quarter of the moon, when the difference between high and low tides is smallest and the eggs are less likely to be washed away.

The migration back to the rain forest takes young crabs around nine days.

Male crabs begin the journey first. Females join slightly later.

**Can you follow the baby crabs back to the rain forest?**

Four weeks after the eggs hatch, tiny crabs emerge from the sea.

Female crabs stand on low cliffs and vibrate their bodies to flick their eggs into the sea. One crab can produce up to 100,000 eggs.

Predators like whale sharks feast on the crab larvae. Millions are eaten, and some years very few survive.

The eggs hatch into shrimplike larvae that go through several growth stages before they become tiny crabs.

Wildebeest are sensitive to changes in atmospheric pressure. Some scientists believe this is why they migrate toward storm clouds. Storms bring rain, meaning grass and water.

Wildebeest are preyed on by cheetahs, lions, hyenas, and wild dogs.

Wildebeest begin migrating north in May or June.

Some 500,000 wildebeest calves are born every year. They are able to run five minutes after they are born.

Up to 450,000 Thomson's gazelle and 200,000 zebra migrate with the wildebeest.

Can you follow the wildebeest herds north?

By December or January, the herds have returned to their southern calving grounds.

# Wildebeest

Wildebeest belong to the antelope family, but look more like small bison. Every year in the Serengeti Plain of East Africa, up to 1.5 million wildebeest migrate north. It is the largest mass migration of mammals on Earth.

The northern Serengeti, where wildebeest feed from September through October, has twice as much rain as the south. It has trees and patches of forest.

Poachers kill around 20,000 wildebeest a year.

Even in the green northern Serengeti, wildebeest exhaust food supplies quickly and need to travel south again.

**Can you follow the herds back to the south?**

Crocodiles wait in rivers to snatch wildebeest as they cross.

Serengeti wildebeest travel up to 2,000 miles/3,200 kilometers a year.

The Mara River is fast and dangerous after rains. Hundreds of wildebeest can be drowned or crushed in the water.

Many calves die in their first year, especially if separated from their mothers.

# Humpback Whales

Humpback whales migrate from the Arctic and Antarctic waters, where they feed, to warm tropical waters, where they have their young. Humpbacks can travel up to 5,600 miles/ 9,000 kilometers in a year — one of the world's longest mammal migrations.

**Can you follow the whale to warmer water?**

Humpbacks can eat up to 2 tons/ 1.8 metric tons of krill a day.

In the final stages of the journey, whales eat little until they reach cold waters where krill is plentiful.

Whales can become tangled in fishing nets or be struck by ships, which may result in injury or death.

In summer, humpback whales feast on krill in colder waters to build up stores of body fat for their journey.

Whales begin their journey when krill travel to the coast for winter.

Some whales stop and rest on the return journey. Hervey Bay, in eastern Australia, is visited by mother whales and calves from July to October.

The return journey is especially dangerous. Adult whales are weaker because they have used up body fat reserves.

Humpback whales, especially young calves, are sometimes attacked and killed by orcas.

Compared to other whales, humpbacks are slow swimmers. Their fastest speed is 16 mph/26 kph, but their average is 2–9 mph/3–14 kph.

Once whales have reached warm waters near the equator, they give birth or mate.

**Can you follow the mother whale and calf back to the feeding grounds?**

In May, the reindeer reach the grassy northern tundra, where they feed. They eat up to 12 pounds/5 kilograms of food a day.

North American reindeer have some of the longest journeys and may travel 3,000 miles/4,800 kilometers in a year.

The Nenets use cone-shaped tents called *mya* or *choom*, which are covered with reindeer hide.

Migrating reindeer can run as fast as 50 mph/80 kph.

They travel in single file, walking in one another's prints to avoid deep snow.

Reindeer head north at the beginning of spring, around March or April.

In winter, reindeer live in forests where they eat lichen. They dig this from under the snow with their scooped hooves.

**Can you follow the reindeer to their summer grazing grounds?**

# Reindeer

Reindeer can be found in the northern regions of Europe, Asia, and North America (where they are known as caribou). Every spring they migrate north to the meadows of the Arctic tundra, where they feast on the nutritious new grasses that grow when winter snow melts.

All reindeer calves are born during a ten-day time period around June. This means that predators can take fewer calves.

Calves can run when they are only a day old.

Some reindeer cross rivers on their journey. This can be dangerous, but reindeer are good swimmers.

**Can you follow the reindeer back to their winter range?**

In September or October, reindeer begin the journey back to the south.

Arctic and gray wolves are the most dangerous predators to reindeer.

Once the reindeer return to their winter range, the annual migration cycle begins again.

Reindeer calves are also preyed on by golden eagles and bears.

# Monarch Butterflies

As winter approaches in North America, a black-and-orange cloud of more than 100 million monarch butterflies leaves the northern parts of the continent to fly south to Mexico and Southern California. It is a migration of up to 3,000 miles/5,000 kilometers and several generations, for the butterflies that return north for summer will be the great-grandchildren of those that migrated south.

**Can you follow the monarch butterflies south before winter?**

In early autumn, monarch butterflies start to head south.

Butterflies can travel around 80 miles/130 kilometers a day or more if the winds are good.

Scientists believe butterflies start migrating due to autumn's shorter daylight hours and falling temperatures.

Before the butterflies migrate south, they gorge on nectar to build up fat reserves.

The butterflies that migrate south do not have fully developed reproductive organs and will not lay eggs until after winter.

Although only one generation makes the southern journey, the journey back to Canada and the northern United States will be completed by several generations of butterflies.

The butterflies lay their eggs in Texas or California's Central Valley, after which they die.

The monarchs sleep until February or March. When they wake they are able to mate. Then they begin the journey north.

They follow the same routes taken by previous butterflies.

**Can you follow the monarch butterflies north now that it is warmer?**

At night, the butterflies swarm on trees to rest. Monarchs have used these trees for generations and may recognize the scent from past migrations.

The butterflies gather in dense orange colonies on trees to hibernate for winter.

Some butterflies winter in Southern California, others in the fir forests of mountainous central Mexico.

# Mali Elephants

In the Gourma region of Mali, in the southwest Sahara desert, a small population of elephants undertakes the longest known elephant migration. They live in an arid landscape and must constantly move around to find food and water.

In the dry months of April and May, elephants can be found at Lake Banzena.

**Can you follow the elephants' path?**

The elephants begin moving south when the rainy season starts around June.

Female elephants and calves travel in herds. Each herd is led by a matriarch — the oldest female.

Male elephants travel alone and often follow a different migration route.

The porte des éléphants (elephant door) is a narrow passage between two rocky ravines that all Mali's elephants pass through.

Mali elephants can endure desert temperatures hotter than 122°F/50°C by day.

Scientists believe there are around 350 Mali elephants left. They are the northernmost herd of elephants in Africa.

Mali elephants are threatened by poachers, who illegally hunt the elephants for their ivory tusks.

In recent years, less rain and a growing human population has increased competition for resources between humans and elephants.

Mali elephants usually make their longer journey at night when it is cooler.

Mali elephants migrate around 300 miles/480 kilometers a year, traveling up to 35 miles/56 kilometers a day.

Around August, elephants cross into the nation of Burkina Faso. This is as far south as they will go.

Now it's the dry season and there isn't much water. Can you follow the elephants back to Lake Banzena?

Can you follow the hummingbirds south?

The birds fly south starting in August to avoid the cold and scarcity of food that winter brings.

Females lay one to three pea-size eggs and feed their young for around three weeks.

Hawks, cats, and even praying mantises can be threats to hummingbirds.

Young hummingbirds make their first journey alone. Once they have learned a route they may follow it every year.

Fewer hummingbirds cross the Gulf of Mexico on the return journey, instead flying south along the coast of Texas.

In eastern North America, male birds put on a dramatic flying and diving display to attract a mate.

Some birds rest on fishing boats or oil rigs.

Many birds cross the Gulf of Mexico — a nonstop flight lasting eighteen to twenty-one hours.

Ruby-throated hummingbirds winter in Mexico and Central America, where the warm weather means lots of blooming flowers.

In January and February the hummingbirds head north. Males depart first, females a few weeks later.

Hummingbirds feast on insects and nectar before their migration. They can double their body weight.

Because hummingbirds are so small, strong winds and rain can be life-threatening.

Can you follow the hummingbirds' journey?

# Ruby-throated Hummingbirds

With a wingspan of only 4 inches/10 centimeters and weighing less than a pencil, these hummingbirds are some of the world's smallest long-distance travelers. Every year they make a 1,000 mile/1,600 kilometer journey across North America. Their wings beat up to fifty-three times a second, making a humming sound.

Straw-colored fruit bats are large, powerful flyers with a wingspan of around 30 inches/ 80 centimeters.

Many bats form colonies in treetops. These can be near waterfalls or loud city streets.

The bats leave their colonies between October and December.

Straw-colored fruit bats are found in the tropical rain forests of sub-Saharan Africa.

A bat can make a round trip of 2,400 miles/ 3,800 kilometers in one year.

**Can you follow the bats to Kasanka National Park?**

# Straw-colored Fruit Bats

Every year between October and December, five million to ten million straw-colored fruit bats travel to Kasanka National Park in Zambia, southern Africa. The bats come to feast on the rain forest fruits, which ripen during the wet season.

In Kasanka National Park,
five million to ten million bats
gather between late October
and December.

In the swamp rain
forests of Kasanka
known as "mushitu," the
bats eat the abundant
ripe fruit. They can
eat twice their body
weight in a night.

Bats can fly 56 miles/
90 kilometers a night.
They rest during the day.

Fruit bats play a vital role in
the swamp forest ecosystem.
They pollinate plants and
disperse seeds.

The bats leave Kasanka
around late December or
early January, when fruit
is no longer available.

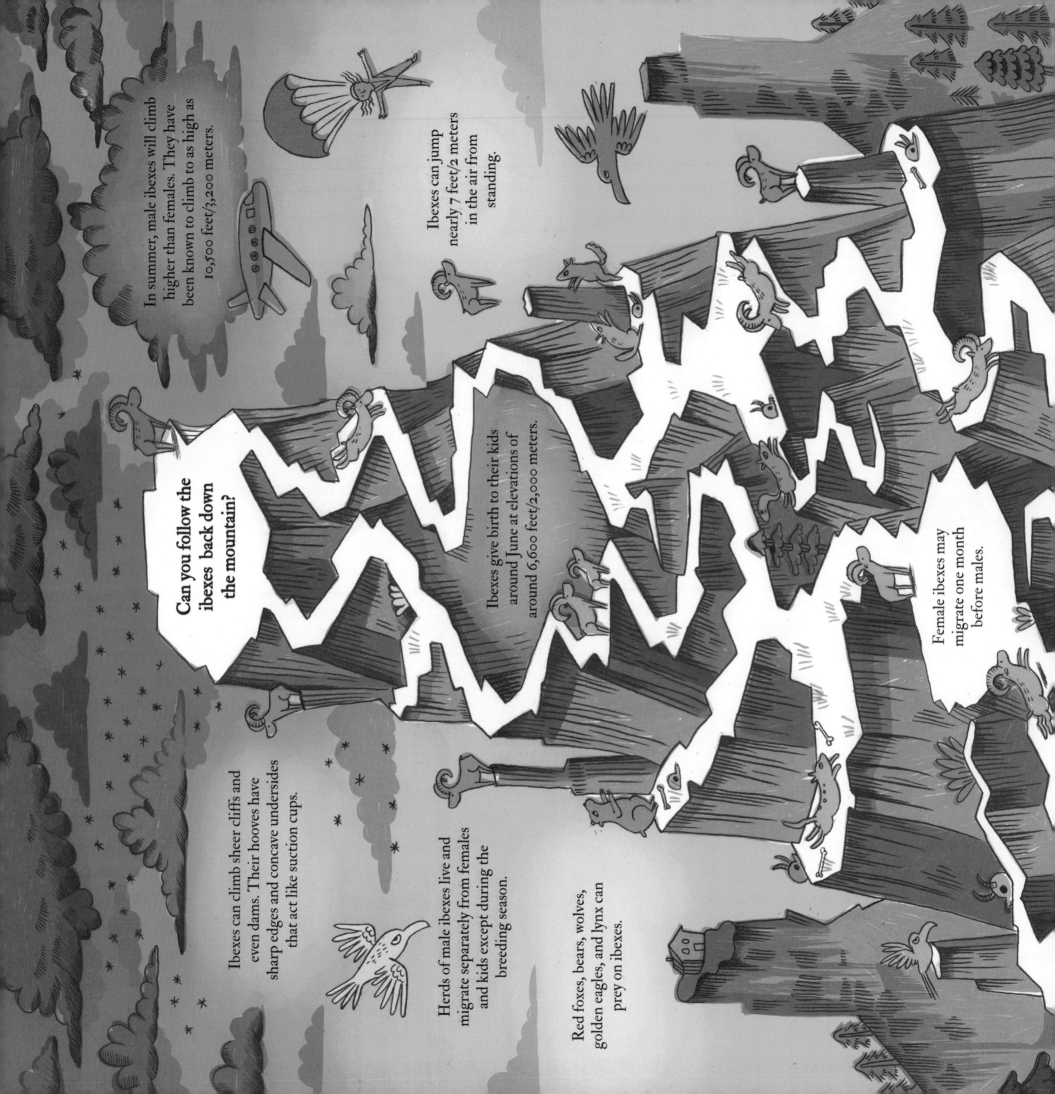

In summer, male ibexes will climb higher than females. They have been known to climb to as high as 10,500 feet/3,200 meters.

Ibexes can jump nearly 7 feet/2 meters in the air from standing.

Can you follow the ibexes back down the mountain?

Ibexes give birth to their kids around June at elevations of around 6,600 feet/2,000 meters.

Female ibexes may migrate one month before males.

Ibexes can climb sheer cliffs and even dams. Their hooves have sharp edges and concave undersides that act like suction cups.

Herds of male ibexes live and migrate separately from females and kids except during the breeding season.

Red foxes, bears, wolves, golden eagles, and lynx can prey on ibexes.

By winter, ibexes have returned to lower elevations.

Newly sprouted plants are the most nutritious. Ibexes migrate up mountains to eat new spring growth.

In winter, alpine ibexes live at elevations as low as 5,200 feet/1,600 meters.

**Can you follow the alpine ibexes up the mountain?**

# Alpine Ibexes

Alpine ibexes can be found in the mountain ranges of central Europe. In winter, they live lower in the mountains, where there is less snow. As spring approaches they climb to higher meadows and rocky slopes, where they graze on the new plants that grow when the snow melts. This is known as altitudinal migration.

# Antarctic Krill

Antarctic krill are tiny shrimplike creatures only around 2 inches/5 centimeters long, but they are the main food source for many animals. As well as migrating with the seasons, krill rise and sink daily from the ocean's surface to deep beneath the waves.

**Can you follow the krill swarm's seasonal journey?**

Krill are the main food source for many Antarctic animals, including whales, birds, seals, and fish.

Krill larvae feed on algae found on the ice.

Between December and March, female krill lay their eggs. These sink 2,600–3,300 feet/800–1,000 meters.

Every winter, adult krill migrate from open water to the Antarctic coast. They often spend winter under pack ice.

Despite their name, crabeater seals consume mainly krill. Their teeth have small points to filter krill from the water.

The huge blue whale can eat up to 4 tons/3.6 metric tons of krill every day.

Once hatched, the immature form of krill, called larvae, swim toward the water's surface.

Krill make up around 95–99 percent of the diet of the chinstrap penguin.

Krill follow a daily migration cycle between the ocean's surface and deep water. This is called diel vertical migration (DVM).

At night, krill feast on phytoplankton near the water's surface.

Can you follow the krill swarm's daily migration?

Krill are vital to the Southern Ocean's ecosystem. They bring nutrients such as iron from deep water into the food cycle.

In summer, krill swarm to the open ocean to feed on microscopic plants called phytoplankton.

Krill return to surface waters about twelve hours after their descent, or when the sun sets.

Every twelve hours, or when the sun rises, krill swarms sink deep beneath the surface to avoid predators.

Krill larvae live under pack ice during the winter.

Some krill migrate as deep as the ocean floor. Here they may eat iron-rich detritus.

# Polar Bears

During winter, polar bears live on the edges of the frozen Arctic ice cap around the North Pole. In summer the pack ice breaks up and drifts away. Bears follow the floes and may even come ashore. During this time, polar bears can travel thousands of miles to find food.

**Can you follow the polar bear south?**

The bears hunt seals by waiting beside breathing holes in the ice and pouncing when the seals emerge.

The flesh and blubber of ringed seals is the main food source of polar bears. They also eat narwhals and walruses.

Polar bears can travel around 31 miles/ 50 kilometers a day.

They can swim long distances between sea ice, but may drown in storms.

When the ice floes break up in summer, polar bears travel for miles to follow the ice and stay with their food source.

If the ice breaks down too much to follow, bears come ashore to find food.

Summer is a hungry time for polar bears. They may eat eggs, geese, plants, or trash left by humans. These are lean pickings for Earth's largest bear, which weighs up to 1,760 pounds/800 kilograms.

The polar bears that travel farthest are those that live the farthest south. In Hudson Bay, Canada, bears come ashore every summer.

In winter, polar bears feast to build up stores of body fat for the summer migration ahead.

Climate change threatens the survival of polar bears, who rely on ice to hunt. Bears today are around 180–200 pounds/80–90 kilograms lighter than they were fifteen years ago.

Can you follow the polar bear back to the frozen north?

Polar bears can lose nearly two pounds/ one kilogram a day during the summer.

Once there is enough ice, polar bears return north. Females in dens do not return until their cubs can travel.

# Rockhopper Penguins

Rockhopper penguins are some of the world's smallest. They spend three to five months at sea before gathering to breed on the small, cliff-lined islands north of Antarctica, from Chile to New Zealand.

Seabirds like the brown skua prey on chicks. Rockhopper penguins protect their nests aggressively.

Around November, female penguins lay eggs, which hatch a month later. Both parents care for the chick.

Rockhopper penguins get their name from their ability to hop up the cliffs where they nest in spring.

The largest rockhopper penguin colony has more than 100,000 breeding pairs.

Penguins return to the oceans in early autumn. Penguins return to the oceans in early autumn. **Can you follow them?**

They may be washed out to sea by waves and have to begin the climb again.

**Can you follow the penguins up, then down the cliff?**

The penguins spend the winter months foraging for food in the ocean. They can even sleep at sea.

They eat krill, squid, and small fish.

The penguins can be eaten by leopard seals and fur seals.

Can you follow the penguins back to their colony?

Around spring, the penguins swim back to their colonies. They return to the same colony every year.

Adult penguins can dive up to 330 feet/100 meters in search of food.

In winter they usually hunt close to their colonies, but they may swim up to 1,200 miles/ 2,000 kilometers away.

# Sockeye Salmon

Sockeye salmon live in both the salty sea and in fresh water. They migrate from the Pacific Ocean up rivers in western North America and the Kamchatka peninsula in Russia to breed. This journey can be as long as 1,500 miles/2,400 kilometers. They find their way to rivers using ocean currents, sunlight, and the earth's magnetic field.

**Can you follow the sockeye salmon to the lake?**

Before sockeye salmon breed, they live in the Pacific Ocean. Their pink flesh comes from the krill they eat.

After two to three years in the sea, the salmon will return to the rivers. Most will go back to the same place they were spawned, which they recognize from the unique chemical makeup of its environment.

Human activity, including fishing and building dams, threatens salmon.

In late spring or early summer, salmon swarm up rivers.

Only 1 to 2 percent of smolts will make it back to the lakes and rivers as adults.

Male salmon change appearance as they migrate. Their jaws become hooked and their backs humped.

Both male and female salmon change from gray-green to bright red.

Several weeks after they have spawned, the salmon die. Bears, wolves, and eagles gather to feast.

Sockeye salmon lay their eggs in autumn. This is called spawning and usually happens in rivers and streams that feed lakes.

**Can you follow the young salmon back to the sea?**

The eggs hatch in winter, and young salmon called fry emerge from their gravel nests in spring.

The salmon can swim against currents and jump up waterfalls.

Brown bears hunt migrating salmon in rivers and lakes.

After hatching, salmon fry may stay in lakes and rivers for one to two years.

In spring, when the snow melts, the young salmon, now called smolts, head downriver to the sea.

# Arctic Terns

Arctic terns are small birds at only 13 inches/34 centimeters long, but they are extraordinary travelers. Every year, terns fly between the Arctic Circle and Antarctica, a journey of 12,400 miles/20,000 kilometers each way. This is one of the longest migrations on Earth. During its life, a tern may travel 1.5 million miles/2.4 million kilometers.

**Can you help the Arctic terns fly south? There are three possible routes.**

Terns that nest in and around Alaska fly south along the Pacific coast.

In the North and South Poles, the sun does not set in summer, when the terns are there. This means terns spend more time in sunlight than any other animal.

In the middle of the north Atlantic Ocean, terns feast on tiny marine organisms called zooplankton as well as small fish.

Terns can travel 240–420 miles/ 390–670 kilometers a day and can sleep while gliding.

The terns will stay around Antarctica for four to five months, feasting on krill.

Adult terns leave Antarctica in early April. While the journey south can take around ninety days, the return journey takes only around forty. This is because the birds make use of different wind patterns.

N

W     E

S

**Can you spot all the animals you've met in this book?**

In July and August every year, terns begin their migration south. This journey takes around ninety days.

Terns that nest in Siberia, northern Europe, southeast Canada, and Greenland fly toward West Africa.

**Choose a path.**

Some birds fly south along Africa's coast, while others fly along the east coast of South America.

Terns weigh around only 4 ounces/ 110 grams. They can glide on the wind without flapping, which saves energy. They may be blown off course.

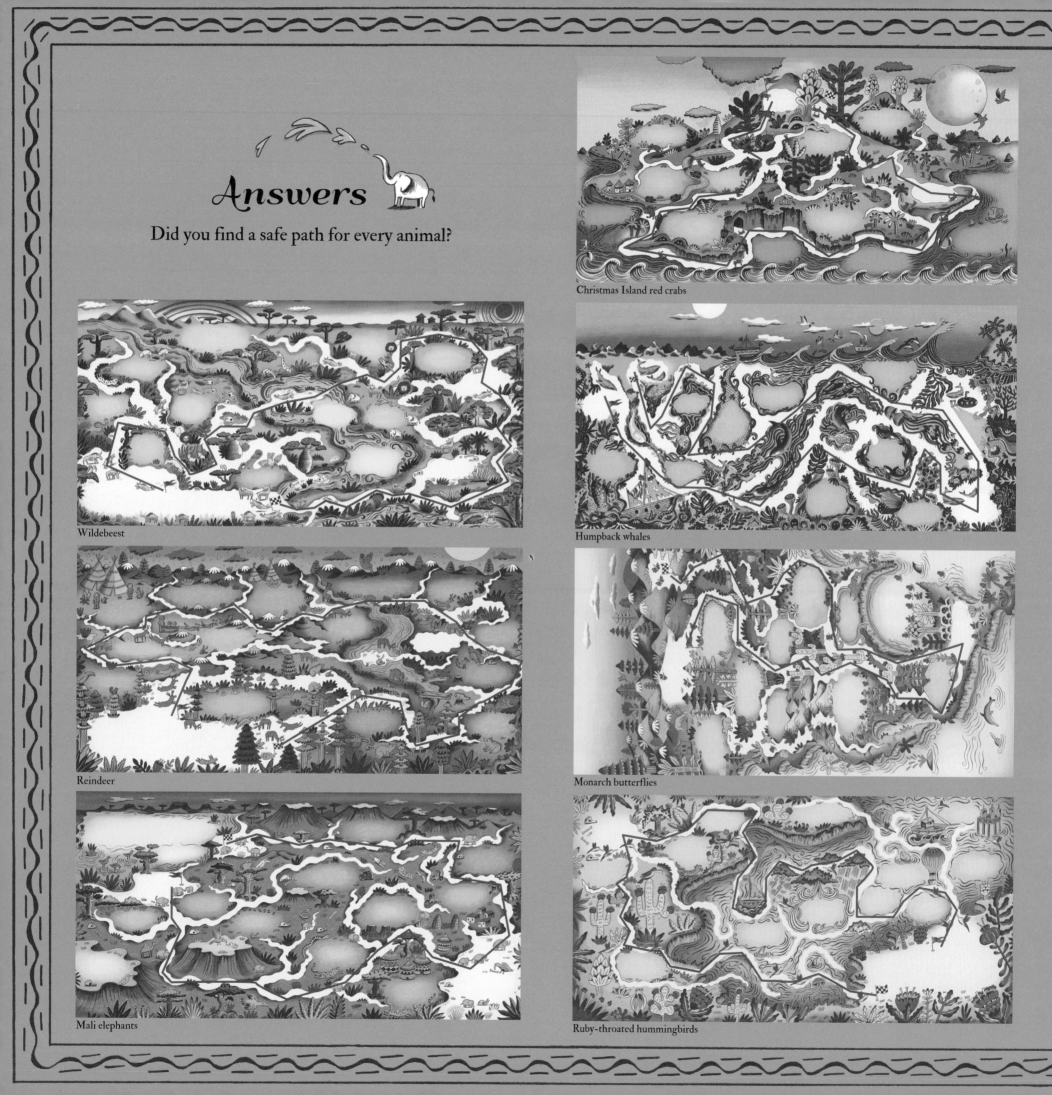

# Answers

Did you find a safe path for every animal?

Christmas Island red crabs

Wildebeest

Humpback whales

Reindeer

Monarch butterflies

Mali elephants

Ruby-throated hummingbirds

Straw-colored fruit bats

Alpine ibexes

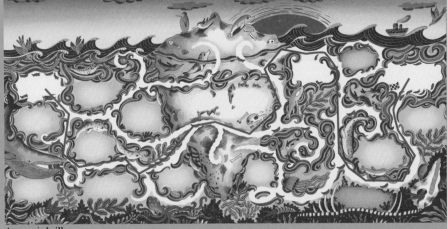

Antarctic krill

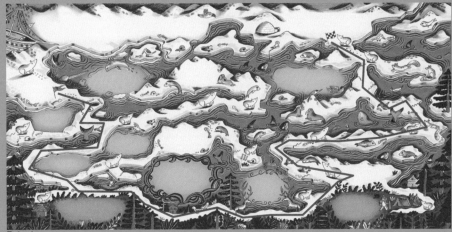

Polar bears

Rockhopper penguins

Sockeye salmon

Arctic terns